The Luftwaffe Guide Book to Basic Survival at Sea

Die Seenotfibel

D. (Luft) 1204

Original text and illustrations by Bruno Jaddatz
Translated from the German by Howard J. Nickel
New verse by Mick J. Prodger

Schiffer Military History
Atglen, PA

Library of Congress Catalog Number: 2001098858.

Printed in China.
ISBN: 0-7643-1619-2

We are always looking for people to write books on new and related subjects. If you have an idea for a book, please contact us at the address below.

Published by Schiffer Publishing Ltd.
4880 Lower Valley Road
Atglen, PA 19310
Phone: (610) 593-1777
FAX: (610) 593-2002
E-mail: Schifferbk@aol.com.
Visit our web site at: www.schifferbooks.com
Please write for a free catalog.
This book may be purchased from the publisher.
Please include $3.95 postage.
Try your bookstore first.

In Europe, Schiffer books are distributed by:
Bushwood Books
6 Marksbury Ave.
Kew Gardens
Surrey TW9 4JF
England
Phone: 44 (0)208 392-8585
FAX: 44 (0)208 392-9876
E-mail: Bushwd@aol.com.
Free postage in the UK. Europe: air mail at cost.
Try your bookstore first.

Foreword

For centuries, rhyme has been used as a means of memorizing and repeating information. Up until the last two hundred years, the majority of people could neither read nor write, and the only way of sharing information among the masses was by word of mouth. By memorizing couplets ending in words with similar sounds, it was easier for the messenger to remember long passages of spoken information. Shakespeare wrote in rhyming verse so that his actors could memorize their lines – most of them being illiterate. Traveling messengers went from town to town spreading news by reciting the rhyming verses they had memorized. Sometimes these verses were set to music by traveling minstrels, and the stories they told took the form of songs which could be learned and repeated, even by children.

Rhyme was also used in the military, where orders and battle tactics were memorized and passed along. Today, troops still chant in verse while marching, although the activity is mostly confined to training and drill exercises.

Die Seenotfibel represents a twentieth century application of an ancient and well-established learning device for memorizing vital, life-saving information.

MJP

Introduction

When first published, this basic survival at sea manual was presented to Luftwaffe airmen in verse which was heavily colloquial and illustrated by colourful cartoon images. The idea was that the novice flyer could memorize the couplets and recall the visual images in order to retain their valuable message.

To preserve the integrity and charm of the booklet, a little poetic license has been taken during translation in order to convey the spirit of the original rhyming form of these important notes. The translators have taken great care to make sure that none of the original, technical meaning has been lost.

Those who appreciate wartime art will undoubtedly enjoy the wonderful, whimsical drawings of Bruno Jaddatz who also composed the original verse.

Students of military aviation history will find the information on survival at sea most valuable. In particular, the drawings, though stylized cartoons, provide extremely accurate renderings of specific items of survival equipment for reference purposes.

MJP and HJN

"It's not like this at the bottom of the sea, read on and learn – and you'll agree!"

Oberkommando der Luftwaffe
Generalquartiermeister

L. In. 16

Brandenburg, den 31. August 1944

Hierdurch wird die Seenotfibel D. (Luft) 1204 genehmigt.

I. A.

Klintzsch

Zeichnungen und Verse: Bruno Jaddatz, Berlin

Flight o'er water's risky, so airmen please take note
and always try to make sure that you pack your rubber boat.
To really gain advantage of a mishap, should you choose it:
be prepared, by making sure you know just how to use it!
For there's one fact upon which you can certainly depend -
get it right the first time - or go in the deep end!
Unless you're fit and ready for a good long swimming date,
read this now and learn it all, before it gets too late.
Deny Neptune another catch, then if it suits your wishes,
return home to your loved ones, instead of to the fishes!

Up 'til now he hasn't even read the opening line,
if he's quick he may be lucky - for now's the crucial time!

Practice makes things perfect, so first try it in the stream,
then the real thing might not seem like such an awful dream.

The crate sinks very quickly so be ready with your knife,
cut loose the long securing rope and hold tight for your life!

The raft begins to drift away - don't let go that line!
As long as you can hold on tight, everything is fine.
Still drifting further with the tide? Which line is in your grip?
The end you're holding may just be the one tied to your ship!

Moonlight shadows are deceiving, so please take extra care –
And never follow sand bars that will lead you to nowhere!

The penetrating cold will gnaw at life's own very roots,
so don't remove your helmet, gloves – nor indeed your boots.
It's a widely known hypothesis that, while you're in the drink,
a suit made up of foam will likely keep you in the pink!

And should the raft land upside down – no need to be concerned,
with energy and skill the boat is eas'ly overturned.
Plant your legs dead centre and grasp firm the turning line,
then pull the rope towards you and soon all will turn out fine.

The sturdy rope-rung ladder is a most essential part –
especially for those who are not experts in the art!

Many tricky situations can be overcome, tis' said –
as long as everyone involved aboard will keep their head!

A war council is needed to decide which way to go,
otherwise, with no direction, your progress will be slow.

In lighter winds the sea anchor will help you hold your course
but as a baling bucket it's a valueless resource.

For simple tears and punctures a repair kit will be found,
enough to plug small leaks aboard and keep your vessel sound.

Upon the realization one will never reach home base,
the landing site below becomes the new home in its place!

Here we see the aerial balloon, nearing full inflation.
How it's done? Exactly as shown in this illustration.

The "organ" is of course a most invaluable addition, assuming someone's out there to receive your "help" transmission!

Hold and check exact position, every hour, for the best.
That's when ships keep radio silence so they'll hear your S.O.S.

To fast is never easy, when it's sustenance you need
but worse, when no one knows about your plight, or lack of feed

Tormenting thirst brings thoughts of morning dew around the boat,
But beer time's when the thirst is 'specially noticed in the throat.

Little Liesle loves the sunshine for a really healthy tan,
but in the raft be careful and avoid it if you can.
With rain however, it's the same for both of you, so try
to think of how to keep it off so you'll stay warm and dry.

The rescue line flies upwards in an ever growing loop –
pulls the solitary swimmer to the safety of the group.

Always keep in mind that this is not a sporting race.
Save energy (and spare your boat!) by slowing down the pace.

One soon can learn the value of a favourable breeze,
Use the sail for making headway with considerable ease.

Is it worthwhile to launch a flare? That now becomes the question.
If someone's there to see it, yes of course - a good suggestion!
But if you're miles from anywhere, alone upon the ocean,
To waste a precious signal flare would be a foolish notion.

Be sure the flame of the hand-held flare points the right way – please take note – so the red-white-red of the signal fire lands a long way from the boat!

To attract a passing pilot, flying by – on sunny days,
The mirror's recommended, for redirecting rays.

No one will be suspicious if the ocean turns to green,
This "urine" in the water will help you to be seen!

When help appears, let all aboard get ready to join in
and draw as much attention so the rescue can begin.
In particular the bright red smoke will signal your distress.
And soon you'll be back home and dry – away from all this mess!

Quax in Distress at Sea

Quax of the Luftwaffe

The character Quax appeared in training/propaganda movies and became popular among Luftwaffe flight personnel for his antics. This is the only known example of a Quax adventure to appear in print, and forms the second part of training manual D. (Luft) 1204 as it was originally published in August, 1944.

Today, it is your turn to meet
Quax the test pilot, smart and neat.
You might say "I know his features –
from movies I have seen, to teach us."
This time, in an ocean setting,
words and drawings, we are getting,
to see what action best is taken,
for survival wet and shaken.

All geared up and properly dressed,
Now he's ready to do his best!
Feeling weighty because of the kit
Quax isn't used to the bulky fit.
Very tricky, for one so vain,
to climb, with dignity, into his 'plane.

"Man", he says "to squeeze in here,
I need a shoehorn, that is clear!"
Still, as he'll find out soon enough –
it's best to be padded with all that stuff!

What's that there – a swarm of bees?
No! – enemy machines he sees!
Plunging in with all his might,
Quax is ready to join the fight.
At least eighty have already fallen
And as he lines up, Quax is callin'
"I'll get you yet" to one more foe,
then dives down on the 'plane below.
Scrap-metal flying, smoke starts to pour–
One more victory to Quax' score!

Suddenly, caught by surprise,
Quax can scarce believe his eyes.
His 'plane is hit and there's no doubt,
no choice, no option – just bail out!
Completely alone and over the sea
"At least my knowledge is good," says he.
For often he'd practiced this situation
and knew what to do for his salvation.

Pressing the buckle above the sea,
he lets his parachute go free.

Quick! Open the air bottle on the vest –
fully inflate, before you rest.

Quax now thinks it's time he oughta
get in his raft and out of the water!
Grasping beneath him – it's quite a knack,
finds the air bottle, still in its pack.
Using his other hand, which is still free,
Twists on the valve and, quite easily,
gas hisses out – not long to wait,
the precious boat starts to inflate.

Suddenly Quax has all kinds of troubles
With the raft inflated his problem doubles!
For if not properly tied down,
it will float away, leaving Quax to drown.
Water ballast prevents capsizing,
shake the bag - quite energizing!

Grabs the raft, now climb on slow –
from the stern is the way to go.
Edges his way on more and more,
grips the handles and hits the floor.

Once aboard – the hard part done
Quax laughs loudly, the battle won.

Topping up the raft by blowing
His confidence now overflowing.
The boat – firm, smooth and round of feature,
like lying on a plump young creature!

The sea anchor, made good and ready
is tossed o'er board, to hold her steady.
With time to think at last Quax ponders –
How will it go, from here, he wonders.

So well prepared is our friend Quax
There's nothing his equipment lacks.
A bag of dye for colourizing
Signal flag for recognizing
Lamp for night time, pistol and flares
(Twelve of them, but use with care),
smoke signal cartridge – and don't forget,
a box of rations, so he's all set!
Quax knows his stuff so well it seems,
He can juggle it, even in his dreams.

Oh lucky Quax, spotted at last.
The first aircraft to fly right past
will save him from his present plight
thanks to the LUX, sea rescue light.
Extra rations from this chance meetin',
are welcome, since his are all eaten!

No question, Quax is full of cheer
Now that rescue's almost here.
"If only I had my heavenly bed,
but no, this cold wet raft instead."

Night time brings this to one's attention –
a fact the manuals neglect to mention!

Many hours later, with rescue arrived,
Quax is happy to know he survived,
reluctant to give up his rubber boat,
his speech takes on a serious note:
"In spite of your encouragement, chaps,
one cannot help wondering if, perhaps,
things will be the same again?"
And in his face, they see his pain.

Soon as he reaches base he'll find,
his fears are groundless – and peace of mind.

His friends are filled with deep emotion,
regaled with stories of the ocean

Cute young girls – all trying their luck –
ask "Didn't you wish for a car or truck?"

Speaking softly, Quax reveals,
"What use would be a set of wheels?"

Courageous deeds may fade – and fast
become mere stories of the past.
We learn of such from history's pages
handed down across the ages.
Next time you glimpse a book of knowledge,
in a library, bookshop, school or college,
be sure to look up "Qu" and note
Quax the Captain of a rubber boat!

Also from the Publisher

Luftwaffe *vs.* RAF: Flying Clothing of the Air War, 1939-1945. *Mick J. Prodger.* An up-close and serious examination of the various patterns of flight jackets, suits, headgear and gloves worn by the courageous pilots and aircrews of these two great adversaries during WWII. This book includes a look at some of the more bizarre and experimental outfits as well as the standard flying kit for different climates and regions, with a special section on electrically-heated clothing. Also examined is the parallel development of flying clothing in the Luftwaffe and the Royal Air Force, and the surprising influence each country had upon the other.
Size: 9"x12" • over 500 color and b/w photographs • 160 pp.
ISBN: 0-7643-0234-5 • hard cover • $49.95

Luftwaffe *vs.* RAF: Flying Equipment of the Air War, 1939-1945. *Mick J. Prodger.* This volume closely examines the development and uses of personal flying equipment of the Luftwaffe and RAF throughout WWII. Compasses secreted in tunic buttons, floating rations, and even suits with built-in parachutes. All types of parachutes and harnesses, life preservers, inflatable boats, survival tools, weapons for self-defense, and even some of the paperwork and personal items carried by the airmen. Study the sophisticated rescue and survival equipment available to Luftwaffe crews, alongside the clever, yet often brilliantly simple devices which enabled so many RAF flyers to evade capture.
Size: 9"x12" • over 500 color and b/w photographs • 144 pp.
ISBN: 0-7643-0249-3 • hard cover • $49.95

Vintage Flying Helmets: Aviation Headgear Before The Jet Age. *Mick J. Prodger.* This new book explores the history and development of early flying headgear throughout the pioneering nations in military and sport aviation, from the earliest exploits of the Wright Brothers, to the end of World War II. Drawn from aviation museums and private collections from around the world, the illustrated color section features over 1000 photographs depicting more than 650 different items of flying headgear: helmets, goggles, oxygen masks and accessories, including many unique personalizations and rarely seen items.
Size: 9"x12" • over 1,000 color and b/w photographs • 336 pp.
ISBN: 0-88740-776-5 • hard cover • $75.00

Gear Up! Flight Clothing & Equipment of USAAF Airmen in World War II. *Jon A. Maguire.* Provides an in-depth examination of personal flight clothing and equipment used by United States Army Air Force flyers in World War II. In addition to U.S. issue items, the book also covers R.A.F. gear used by American airmen. The original items are presented in full color photographs, including detail shots and labels. Also included are hundreds of World War II era photographs showing the items in use, as they were worn. Portions of actual USAAF instructional manuals are provided as well. A valuable reference to historians, collectors, and modelers.
Size: 8½"x11" • over 600 b/w and color photos • 184 pp.
ISBN: 0-88740-744-7 • hard cover • $45.00

Pilots' Information File 1944: The Authentic World War II Guidebook for Pilots and Flight Engineers. The Pilots' Information File (PIF) was the standard reference for any general information required of USAAF pilots and flight engineers. The PIF covered items of a general nature that a combat flyer must know in order to fight an air war and survive.
Size: 8½"x11" • photographs, drawings, diagrams • 268 pp.
ISBN: 0-88740-780-3 • soft cover • $19.95

Eagles Recalled: Pilot and Aircrew Wings of Canada, Great Britain and the British Commonwealth 1913-1945. *Warren Carroll.* These pieces of cloth and metal symbolize the daring, bravery, suffering and loss of men who flew in deadly aerial battles for democratic freedom. Much of the material contained in this publication has never been published. The author has also made new historical discoveries presented here for the very first time – he has accessed private collections, photographed rare museum acquisitions, and received support from historians in seven countries over a period of some ten years. This work brings to readers a detailed and comprehensive study of the brevets issued to aviators who fought with Great Britain in World Wars I and II.
Size: 8½"x11" • over 800 color and b/w photos • 240 pp.
ISBN: 0-7643-0244-2 • hard cover • $79.95